The Written Word

Word

My Legacy

Poetry by
Bootsie Lauridsen

IMPERIUM PUBLISHING
CREATE YOUR STORY

The Written Word

ISBN: 978-1-64318-072-4

IMPERIUM PUBLISHING

1097 N. 400th Rd
Baldwin City, KS, 66006
www.imperiumpublishing.com

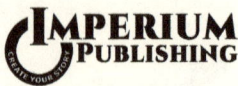

These words were put together on special occasions when feelings were unyielding and spoken words inadequate, and are meant to be shared with anyone who cares to know of these times.

This book belongs to

_____

I have been a daughter, a wife, and then after 55 years, a widow. As a mother, I have been blessed with three sons and one daughter who, in turn, blessed me with ten grandsons, four granddaughters, and two great-granddaughters. My VITA, though it might be unnecessary, begins when I graduated from high school in 1955 from Fairmont High School in Minnesota. I attended Gustavus Adolphus in St. Peter, Minnesota for two years before I married Monty Lauridsen in 1957. Returning to college some years later, I graduated with a Bachelor of Science from Baker University in 1976.

Strike Three, You're Out!

Spare me a minute to tell you of my resisting a strong urge to get a dog. Instead of rescuing a dog (I really am not quite ready), I have decided to volunteer at the Lawrence Humane Shelter walking and socializing dogs, and getting my canine fix. Seemed simple enough as I'm in Lawrence to see Monty every other day. I took the volunteer training, and today, I packed my poop shoes, dog treats, volunteer form, and arrived with a "do good" feeling. Inside, I proudly said. "I'm here to walk a dog." They very nicely told me Monday wasn't a volunteer day. Strike one!

I did read EVERYTHING, but guess they probably didn't think so and wondered what else I did not get. But the director, a character herself, noted it was a nice day, and a dog would love a walk. I liked her attitude about rules.

Which dog to pick? They are all barking, and most are BIG and mean-looking. Many have signs on their kennels ... "STOP...is not evaluated for handling yet," or "DON'T WALK." I did remember reading that I should start out small, but small was not to be found—they're adopted quickly. Just big and strong and jumping and barking/begging dogs that scare the bejusus out of folks. Mainly lab and pit bull mixes, and hunting dogs eager for the field. So I picked a somewhat calm lab mix which I found out was in the puppy section. Guess he was calm to save energy, and he was the biggest damn pup I've ever seen.

I got the slip collar on him, and he immediately jumped on me. He was not a small puppy, and I could only take him to the puppy pens which were small and not interesting him much. He spent a lot of time jumping on me, and I spent a lot of time making him stay down. I guess that is the socializing they keep talking about.

He was indeed a puppy because his nails were razor sharp, and he gave me a good gash across my wrist and several scrapes on my hands and arms. After about 15 minutes, I took him back in and had to sheepishly ask for a sink in which to lick my wounds, now fearing dog feces and God knows what else in my bloodstream. And I signed a waver. The director gave me some good ointment and a band aid. I asked for another time at bat, and went back for more. What a trooper. Strike two!

I chose a long-legged (that gave me pause, but she wasn't mean looking) fox hound/mix with a nice bay. I opened the door and found that she didn't want out enough to let me put the collar on her. Well, you can't get a collar on a dog that doesn't want it on while reaching through an 8-inch opening of the kennel door. So, of course I went in. Whoops … when the door shuts, so does the latch. So there I was, locked in a kennel for my last at bat. Luckily, I still have a few problem-solving skills, and noticed that there was a loop on the slip leash. After a couple of tries, I hooked the latch and pulled it up. Next problem, getting the collar on her before she got out the door, but I guess my presence in her kennel was daunting enough that she let me slip it on. She really wasn't too glad to be out, but she walked around the pen without my having to pull her, and after about a half an hour we had an intimate moment as I sat on a bench. When we started back in, she was like a horse when you turn them toward home. She couldn't go fast enough. Obviously, she felt safe in her kennel. Strike three!

So, my urge to have a dog was greatly diminished after my first day volunteering at the shelter, but I know when I find that medium-sized, short haired mutt that looks me in the eyes from her kennel and says, "I like you," you'll be reading about my new dog in my Christmas letter. (2020, "I didn't.")

Thanks for letting me share these things with you. Remember, my sharing partner, bless his soul, is not here.

March 17, 2009

The Seasons

1993-94

"I see God in Nature and notice His gifts each month."

January

A new period begins. We seek renewal,
    resolve to be better and to conquer our failings.
But soon everything is as before.
    How can life be ever-changing, yet the same?

Flat-bottomed vessels, blades and runners
    carry eager travelers on playful journeys.
Wraps spread to dry on kitchen floors,
    ensure other trips will be taken.

Drawn curtains cozily enclose us
    in our winter cocoons.
Gridiron contests and relaxing pastimes
    fill these shortened days.

Venture outside and behold the vividness.
    Day or night, the scene is striking.
This harsh, icy season is softened
    by its beauty and the promise it imparts.

February

Red hearts signify vibrance and warmth
    which are visibly absent.
We must look inward for beauty and passion.
    This is the season of love.

The outer world is colorless and unexpressive.
    Gray describes our domain at rest.
Dreariness thrives!

We lock ourselves in, dusting off
    our passive diversions,
awaiting the passage of this shortest period.

Every fourth year an extra day lengthens the wait,
    readjusting man's calendar to the natural one.

We honor loved ones and national patriots,
    and yearn for Spring's artist to color
our existence once more.

March

Yards and skin are bared.
    Flowers emerge, urged by the sun.
But, beware the bitterness yet to come.
    Spring teases!

Doors are opened to sounds of humanity
    and wind chimes clatter.
Soon the sun will rise centered in our road
    and late enough to be witnessed.

Emerald hues proclaim Irish folk lore
    and the earth's renewal.
New life abounds—the universe awakens,
    and a new grandson is born.

Our hearts are full!

April

Breezes scatter seeds and sweet odors,
    stirring sensuality in all domains.
Rains surprise us, often from angry skies,
    coloring the earth and cheering our dreary souls.
Gardens falsely beckon,
    but frost worries the eager heart.
Feathered guests leave or take up residency,
    and Orion lounges in his western sky room.
An hour of time evaporates
    as Man creates his own timetable.
Uncle Sam picks our pockets
    or accepts our gifts, depending on our perspective.

Our souls are renewed!

May

Noisy mowers and blossomy fruit trees
    announce that Spring is really here.
Insects creep and fly into our world,
    reminding us we are not omnipotent.

The density of tree seeds that carpet
    the ground and clog rain spouts
indicate the weather of the coming season.
    How do trees know what we do not?

Plants awakening from Winter naps
    are introduced to their fragile annual cousins
whose brilliance can be shared only once.
    What makes the difference between them?

We honor motherhood, the beginning of life,
    and celebrate commencement, the close of school life,
and decorate our cemeteries, memorializing the end of life.

The Alpha and the Omega!

June

Skinny-necked nestlings squeal for tidbits
    they will soon find on their own.
The quickness of the fledge amazes me,
    but the necessity does not – predators await!

Billowy white clouds drift across the bluest skies
    on gentle breezes that envelop us in comfort.
Sticky-legged bugs bang into our lighted windows,
    and captured fireflies grace many a child's nightstand.

Cultivating, mulching, pruning—preparation now
    to sustain life for the season to come.
It is fitting we honor fathers,
    who spend their lives preparing and sustaining.

Rainfall is crucial to what will be,
    and children sneak to get wet in forbidden places.
Lawn chairs are dusted and camping gear aired
    as we take up residence out-of-doors.

Perfect days and perfect nights!

July

Heat shimmers relentlessly, and skies are dry.
  We flee to escape in carefree diversion.
Family reunions, vacations, weekend retreats—
  everyone goes somewhere.

Sounds of play float across the waters,
  and city pools host gleeful splashing.
Even thirsty bees frequent the bird baths.
  Water sustains us.

Our gaze turns up to bright bursts and blooms
  in rousing celebration,
while our minds think back with reverence
  to the great Declaration.

Oft-used picnic tables are laden with
  fried chicken, sweet corn and watermelon.
At dusk, cicadas remind us
  that Autumn approaches.

The playful season concludes!

August

Sultry dog days slow us down
    as we try to finish summer tasks.
Darkness comes earlier to chase to heat,
    and crops yellow in weedy rows.
School bells toll, bringing dread
    to all but the social farm child.
Pollen is on the fly,
    promoting life and stuffing noses.
Birds gather –
    awaiting their inner signal to flee.
We celebrate our life together
    on the twenty-fourth day.

Change is in he air!

September

Does the sky just seem bluer,
    images breathtaking against it?
Locusts, cicadas, crickets, school bells
    knell the death of summer.
Labor, life's obligation, is recognized
    with an ironic day off.
One-eyed storms rage over oceans
    as the battle between warm and cool begins.
Spider strands from unknown places
    span our walkways.
Birds cluster on land and water
    signaling their instinctive journeys.
Cool morns, eves, and perfect days
    chase the heat just in time.
Jack Frost prepares his easel
    to begin his Fall portrait.

This is a favored month!

October

Leaves, fulfilling their final purpose,
    drift across the scene.
Crisp, invigorating air and warm colors
    belie the cold, restful season to come.

Creatures, instinctively gathering, hiding
    and scurrying in preparation,
remind us of our kinship as we
    harvest our crops and shut our windows.

Pumpkins sporting unlikely faces
    and strange beggars on our doorstep
mark the passage of this lunar period.

I feel tranquil as I witness Autumn's
    gifts, and I am glad that I notice them.

November

Cheerless gray clouds, hidden by early
    dusk, air smelling of burned leaves
signal the end of what has been.

Birds quiver as reports of doom
    rip the air. They check for backyard
hand-outs and fill the sky with
    noisy patterns.

The harvest is complete, feasts are
    prepared in gratitude and the
land is prepared.

The season of rest is upon us!

December

Our souls stir in anticipation
    yet the holiday season comes too soon.
Vows are made to keep in balance
    what is expected and what should be.

Scarcely noticed is Winter's nature,
    stark bareness one day, snowy cover the next.
Protection means survival,
    fur thickens, leaves cover, food stored, mittens found.

Do we note the beauty of a cardinal in the snow,
    the serenity of a moonlit Winter night,
the eternal glimmers on high,
    the universe beyond the colored lights?

As the close, New Year awaiting,
    we reflect on love and hope.
The emerald wheat, peeking through the snow,
    foretells the season of renewal.

The Grandchildren

Individuals, yet fragments of ourselves!

The Grandchildren

They enter our lives, ready or not—
    little fragments of our genes.
In their households they're a humble lot,
    at our home they're Kings and Queens.

But even royalty needs to learn
    they can't have every whim.
Therefore we teach them the need to earn,
    and spoil in the interim.

With these offspring come worry and cheer,
    just as it was with our own.
And whether we watch from far or near,
    we're pleased that our seeds are sown.

2000

Brian – 10 years

So social and kind—
Those eyes, always darting, looking
    for an adventure.
Feelings, worn on his sleeve, show
    kindness to all living things

Erik – 9 years

So wise and sensitive—
Those eyes, always watching, knowing
    your every thought.
Feelings, deep inside, struggle to
    come out and mingle and be understood.

Kyle – 7 years

So curious and creative—
Those eyes, always questioning,
    seeking reasons and opportunities.
Feelings, often hidden, are expressed
    freely in the world of imagination.

Adam – 7 years
> So tender and active—
> Those eyes, averted in shyness,
> > belie a hidden strength.
> Feelings, sometimes erupt, requesting
> > individuality or showing love.

Randi – 6 years
> So sweet and helpful—
> Those eyes, always boring right into
> > your heart, invite affection.
> Feelings, cautiously shared, reveal
> > sentimentality and care for others.

Cory – 5 years
> So carefree and loving—
> Those eyes, always twinkling, reveal
> > a love of fun and a little mischief.
> Feelings, quick to surface, show a
> > struggle to hold his own, yet be himself, the youngest.

Ryan - 4 years

So quiet and accepting—
Those eyes, filled with wonder as
    they watch and learn
Feelings, held within this gentle spirit,
    surprise you, when shared, with candor.

Ben - 4 years

So happy and talkative—
Those eyes, bursting with laughter
    as they converse with yours.
Feelings, willingly expressed, show concern
    for others, but also a need to be alone.

Aaron - 1 year

So wary and shy—
Those eyes, hidden on mama's chest
    so they can't be challenged by strangers.
Feelings, in this stage, express the desire
    for the familiar with which he is happy.

Tyler – 3 months

So content and alert—
Those eyes, trusting as they focus on
    familiar sights and sounds.
Feelings, driven at this time by basic needs,
    can not tell us what he will be.

Jayna – 15 years

So generous, thoughtful and aware—
Those eyes, dark and deep as a raven's
    always buried in a book or seeking
    her beloved friends.
Feeling, kept to herself unless she
    shares he radiant smile.

Kayti – 12 years

So thoughtful and insightful—
Those eyes, always seeing the
    essence of all around her with
    clarity and wisdom.
Feeling, held in check behind her
    smile, but shared freely with animals.

Kristoffer – 11 years

So diligent and inquisitive—
Those eyes, always focused on
    the task at hand, seeking
    perfection and reward.
Feeling, on the surface, but deeply seated
    in caring for others and doing the right thing.

Sashi – 11 years

So spirited and affectionate—
Those eyes, dark and impish,
    sizing you up, demanding
    interaction and stealing your heart.
Feeling, complex and ever changing
    to keep up with her energetic life.

Great Grand Daughters

Kayden – 12 years
> So capable and compassionate—
> Those eyes, watching all around her
> > and reading sheet music for her violin.
> Feelings, cautious, not easily shared,
> > but comfortable with peers and
> > guiding her wisely.

Emma – 7 years
> So spunky yet sweet—
> Those eyes, full of fun, and loving fast cars
> > from early on, thanks to her Papa, and
> > can recognize a Lamborghini from a Bugotti.
> Feelings, carried on her sleeve so there's
> > no guessing, and friends come easily.

Random Thoughts

Luck of the Draw

Life is a high stakes poker game
 with DNA dealing the cards.
We can't pick our table or always the players.
 Our only hope is to play our cards well.
Hands are opened with anticipation,
 and chances taken with promise.
Strategies go for naught when bluffs fail,
 and the rules aren't the same for all.
Some hands reveal merely a Pair.
 (necessities of life)
Some sport a Full House.
 (love and contentment)
Rarely, we experience a Royal Flush.
 (ecstasy and passion)
Sometimes we face nary a pair.
 (fear, doubt, pain and disappointment)
The ultimate challenge—knowing when to fold,
 putting others first and giving of oneself.
And, when to stay,
 honoring our desires and protecting the Self.

August 1994

Winners know the Answer!

The Golden Thread

In the late 1960s and early 1970s,
    the Baker community wove a common golden thread
which bound our spirits and kept us connected.

The thread was stitched through the fabric of time,
    knotting each time our lives touched.
With each knot, the tether was strengthened.

Strands of ideas, experiences and memories
    dangled between the knots,
reaching into our individual worlds.

The ends of this cord were joined in reunion, May, 1994.
    The thread was woven around a core of love and respect,
which ensured our existence in Camelot.

June 1994

Dr. Neal Malicky included the following at President Doty's funeral service and read the poem above: "There was a reunion of Baker folks in 1994, 20 years after Jim and Merciel left Baker. (Think for a minute how unusual that is for a college to do.) Bootsie Lauridsen said, 'They made Baker a special place for all of us that has never been duplicated.' She shared her thoughts in a poem."

To My Husband

What is this thing called love,
    This term we use so loosely?
They say that love is blind,
    unconditional, everlasting.
They say that love is trust,
    commitment, patience, forgiving.
The poets are amiss,
    for love is only a word.
A word to describe a feeling,
    that is simply without definition.
A definition we attempt as
    the feeling is so powerful.
So powerful that it binds
    when there is no explanation.
No explanation for the bond we have,
    but I say its love, my Husband.

Your Wife, Bootsie
February 14, 1995

Realist to Poet

Wheat is all this creative blather?
Live in the real world, I would rather.
Where black is black not degrees of gray.
Where words are words meaning what they say.

To search and search the clever word
seems to me totally absurd.
Please state it clearly, what you mean,
just subjects and verbs, nice and clean.

I don't grasp your need to express
artistic terms to souls undress,
to catch my eye so I might see
the feeling realm from which I flee.

January 1996

Written for poetry class as an example of persona.

Walnut Valley Festival

If you've ever been there, come September,
your soul stirs to pickin' and fiddlin'.
Winfield beckons—

Through the gate, wristband on, your senses are alerted,
a sea of camps, funnel cakes, onions and catfish grilling.
Mountain music drifts—

Camps are chaotic, tolerant, and cramped.
Flags, banners, smoke mark sites.
The pecan grove, treasured—

A diverse crowd with a common passion,
hippies, yuppies, hillbillies, elders gather.
Audience and performers, interwoven—

The listeners scour the program and fold it just right,
new sounds, old favorites, workshops are marked.
Lawn chairs, toted—

Music makers perform in camp or on stage
jamming in camaraderie, day and night.
Instruments required—

T-shirts and hats proudly display
whims, causes, and festivals past.
Affiliation, paraded—

Fanny packs in positions that belie their name,
boots, tie dye, braids and bottled water are in.
Musical correctness, upheld—
Acoustically best are chosen and honored.
Unlike in style and sound, they compete.
The festival's heart, endured—

Approval bursts from four makeshift stages,
foot stompin', knee slappin', hand clappin', yeahs.
Campground performances improvised—

At Stage I, car tops reflect sun, mimicking spotlights.
The moon rises to the strains of A Flat train whistles.
Bluegrass indoors, ruined—

Headed home with the Monarchs, feet still tappin',
honking at one another, WVF bumper sticker waving.
A common experience, hailed—

October, 1994

Published in Walnut Valley Official Program – September 1995

*Monty and I went to many Walnut Valley Bluegrass festivals. We took our
camper and stayed for several days.*

Marriage

How can it be that marriage works
    when frailty and failure lurks
in shadows of inflated egos,
    hopes and unfulfilled libidos?

Who is the boss, and who is not?
    One patient soul does help a lot.
Equal duties can't be achieved
    as modern couples once perceived.

But, when there's love and tender touch,
    all those concerns don't matter much.
Commitment made to give and take
    a lasting bond and marriage make.

November 1995

Written for the wedding shower of a friend.

La Monte I. Lauridsen

I've thought and thought of how to sum
this man of sixty years.
Words are wanting and hard to come,
he has so many tiers.

His human side is firm but fair,
he sees beyond his sphere.
Deep feelings are expressed with care,
intrusion is a fear.

His thinking side's beyond reproach,
a quest to understand,
and then once learned, he's bound to teach
with logic well in hand.

Spiritually, he's not pious,
but moral and decent,
acting on belief, not bias,
his soul's honest comment.

And all those tiers left undefined,
that make him what he is,
prudence, goodness and sense entwined
do leave a tread that's his.

Your wife, Bootsie
January 1996 for his 60th birthday

Man's Illusion

Ah Man, you super being,
unlocking Nature's secrets
with speed that mocks the millenniums,
offering gifts of comfort and time.
Your mind is the key.

Ah Man, you foolish one,
setting yourself apart,
embracing an illusion of power.
No more essential than plankton,
contemplate nature, and be humbled.

January 1996

Fall Poem

Summer at auction.
Mother Nature's calling the bids.
Going, going, gone!

The Grand Experience

Viewing a picture of the Grand Canyon
    on a sunny day,
this awesome place of God's creation—
eons in the making—
tells stories in the strata
revealing earth's secrets.

This multi-colored masterpiece
from God's magnificent palette,
reveals pinks, purples and golds
peeking around clefts and shadows.

This silent splendor,
where ragged earth meets sky,
defines vastness and solitude
and humbles humanity.

February 1996

With the help of poetry class members.

*We did get to the Grand Canyon in 2001 – hike down the north side, Stayed
at a lodge and then hiked up the south side.*

No School – Snow Day

A sweet message can a phone call bring,
a day at home from a welcome ring.
A gift of unforeseen, unplanned time,
a leisure paradise most sublime.

A tinge of guilt passes through our minds,
a charge we feel to bust our behinds.
A decree of reprieve sets us free.
A thanks to all the powers that be.

January 18, 1996
(on such a day)

The Gift

I happened to notice at last year's visit,
that your jewelry bag was not exquisite.
Now I'm gonna sound like a snobby old hag.
But really, dear sister, a Ziploc bag?
In shame I wanted to turn my back.
Did she bring her clothes in a paper sack?
I vowed then and there to get you a nice case,
so in future unpackings, you could show your face.

1996

Poem was sent to my sister, Ellen, with an ivory, satin, jewelry bag purchased with love.

Could This Child Be You?

I'm at that in-between time.
Not child yet not grown up.
I still play in dirt and grime.
But now can stay cleaned up.

Mom and Dad now look at me
and say I'm growing fast.
I can't wait to older be.
They want the child to last.

School is changed, a real new scene,
there's so much more to learn.
Teachers say to use my bean.
It makes my stomach churn.

Learning how to face a jam,
to rat I'd rather die.
I'm finding out who I am,
where I fit in and why.

I'm more and more on my own,
overnights, secrets told,
clean my room, and use the phone,
always to friendships hold.

Keep my feelings to myself,
so many of them new.
Put my toys upon a shelf,
my childish ways are through.

March 1996

Written for Mrs. Roberts' 6th grade class and 6th graders everywhere.

The Olympic "B" lame

Coke, et. al. started each race,
    finished them too, self possessed.
IBM fell on its face,
    and Atlanta failed the test.

NBC stuck us with "stuff,"
    forgot what we yearned to see.
Updates, clips and boring fluff,
    misused the might of T.V.

When IOC gave up control,
    the Olympic spirit was sold.
It seemed to the world, as a whole,
    the Ugly American took gold.

July, 1996

On the circumstances of the Summer Olympics at Atlanta when the corporate world ran the show.

Repression

Why can't a gal swear like a Tar,
    when other words just won't fit?
As when she just can't start her car,
    there's no better word than shit.

OR when she's just been called a bitch
    just barely overheard.
She needs to scratch the verbal itch
    and say our loud, "Bastard!"

Some think it makes her less demure,
    opened doors she would not earn.
Helluva note I think for sure,
    so I'll stick to shucky durn.

July 1996

Written in the car on the way to Storm Lake, Iowa from Red Wing, Minnesota.

Recognition

C.E.O.s and C.P.A.s,
busy, hectic, empty days,
no lives to touch in urgent ways—
the private sector, boy it pays.

Teachers on the other hand,
working to young minds expand,
underpaid and undermanned—
the public world, ain't it grand?

Those of us who work with you,
know most people have no clue,
the magnitude of what you do—
you change the world, and that is true.

May 1996

Written for BJHS teachers on Teacher Day and for those dedicated souls everywhere.

Beloved Pomona

You showed me where the thrashers walked.
    I told you when my troubles stalked.
We shared secrets, beloved friend.

You showed me walkways full of life.
    I felt humbled in joy and strife,
We shared souls, beloved teacher.

You showed me Nature's inner calm.
    I took its presence as a balm.
We shared peace, beloved healer.

You showed me nothing stays the same.
    I witnessed change when seasons came.
We shared truths, beloved Scholar.

You showed me much if I did look.
    I gave much less than I took.
We shared essence, beloved Pomona.

August 1996

1st place at GFWC of KS poetry contest.

Camping at Pomona State Park was my place of refuge.

Thoughtful Plugger

My opinions wee rarely sought,
    perhaps too quickly given.
Rational thinking went for naught,
    my feeling side was driven

Conversations were safely spent,
    on things of daily dealings.
My husband read with wise intent,
    I wrote to share my feelings.

When he was aroused by someone
    with views he found quite zealous,
I wished I could be that person,
    and found myself quite jealous.

So, when I didn't fill that need
    (Can't all be mental sluggers),
I took listening as my creed
    and joined the thoughtful Pluggers.

February 1997

Father Cod

My love to you, you modest Swede,
　　　blue-eyed and silver-haired.
You are so much a part of me,
　　　though not through bloodline shared.

I often miss your soft-spoke words,
　　　wit, wisdom, and the such.
And as I age, I listen hard
　　　so's not to lose so much.

I know how deep your feelings flow,
　　　you listen and reflect.
Intensity is hidden there
　　　where no one would suspect.

I think you have a hidden drum,
　　　rebel-like free spirit.
But with responsible purpose,
　　　you don't even hear it.

I've heard you say you'd love to live
　　　forever, were it so.
Alas, it wouldn't be much fun
　　　for no one would you know!

April 1997

Written for his 85th birthday.

Once In a Lifetime

What a sight to the upturned eye,
    a fuzzy scene in the darkened sky.
A sky so steady through the years,
    notice comes when the comet nears.

A spotlight on a clear Spring night,
    the tail its beacon, shedding light.
Warmed by the sun, it makes its pass
    with vapor trails of dust and gas.

From Hale and Bopp its name did burst,
    as they were men to see it first.
Last time it came was ages past.
    My lifetime must its image last.

May 1997

During the visit of the Hale-Bopp Comet.

The Ship of Sadness

The ship of sadness visits me,
    an unwelcome, painful stop,
on waters that were trouble free
    'till life's woes did all stir up.

It's thrust on waves of circumstance
    whose course I cannot vary.
It drops the plank, I must advance,
    and it carries me away.

As we sail in the darkened night
    on seas brimmed with salty tears,
the ship of sadness drifts toward light,
    and dawn comes to ease my fears.

Summer, 1997

Mom

I altered her life forever—
    as first born endlessly do,
and now know what that meant for her
    from an old and wiser view.

Though early times were difficult,
    with determined strength her vow,
she focused on the best result.
    Optimistic then as now.

Born to brains and traits quite arty,
    she danced, sang, acted and read.
To this day she loves a party
    and's compelled to plan ahead.

Organization is her thing.
    Everything has its own place.
Boxes with all that's worth keeping,
    labeled and tucked in their space.

Some may declare it stubbornness.
    I say she knows her own mind,
and given not to pettiness.
    She's tolerant, wise and kind.

Cleaning the house holds no appeal.
    It's people that gratify.
Her specialities are made with zeal.
    Shrimp salad and cherry pie.

Desires and ambitious ways,
       unselfishly put aside,
were fulfilled in much later days.
       Her law degree earned with pride.

Her family is her passion.
       She never misses a date.
Birthday, marriage, graduation
       she helps us celebrate.

She taught me how to place a fork,
       to properly make a bed,
and to thoroughly cook the pork,
       to write thanks and knead the bread.

Made me feel I could do all things.
       I know now that isn't true.
But it helped me give things a fling
       at finding what I could do.

My mother can not be defined
       in a chosen word or two.
Our characters are so entwined
       that choosing's hard to do.

But try I do to choose the words
       that fit her like a glove,
afraid that they would go unheard,
       these tangible terms of love.

January 1998

On the occasion of Mom's 80th birthday, January 19, 1918

Walkin' to School

Every day I walk to school,
I go the same old way.
Some may think it's not so cool,
but here is what I say.

I might see a dandelion,
a stalkin' in the grass.
I'd stoop down where it's hidin',
and pick it for my class.

I might see a plastic cup,
a lyin' in disgrace.
I would stop to pick it up,
and use it for a vase.

I might see a butterfly,
a sign of luck you know.
It just seems to flutterby,
no special place to go.

I might hear a noisy bird
a scoldin' in a tree.
Wonder if a foe he heard,
or was it just old me?

I might hear the wind arise,
a rustlin' all the leaves.
Through the branches down it dives
to whip my jacket sleeves.

I might see a mushroom sprout
atop a hefty stalk.
After rains, the worms come out
to wiggle on the walk.

I might learn a lot of things,
a lesson every day.
Walkin' to school knowledge brings
of things along the way.

2001

Won 1st place at 2nd Dist GFWC of KS creative writing contest.
Won 1st place at State GFWC contest.
Won 3rd place at GFWC International convention

A Day in March

This fine March day, I opened the door
    and let the outside in.
For months I've shut out the Frosty hoar,
    but now we're joined again.

The sounds, warm breezes flow into my world,
    and nights begin to fade.
Urgency in my soul is unfurled.
    Time to get out the spade.

March 2004

Super Cookie Limerick

This valentine cookie I bring
for the annual chocolate fling.
Take it, and freeze it.
Cut it, and share it,
or just eat the whole doggone thing.

2000

I always made super cookies for the Annual Chocolate Auction.

Madness

March Madness fits this time of year
for much more than basketball cheer.
The Irish go bonkers,
north go the honkers,
and potholes from nowhere appear.

March 8, 2001

Special time for our family contest

A Walk in Your Shoes

Society should come and stay
    in your classroom for a day,
no hour lunch, no mega pay
    no real product to display.
Demanding guidelines to obey,
    everything is due today.
A lot of knowledge to convey
    to your student's real dismay.
When disruptions impede the way,
    the best of plans go astray.
But the skill and care you portray,
    would make it obvious that day.
"Teachers are saints," they would say.

For Teacher Day 1999

Christmas Time

Seasons Greetings

This year came, this year went,
    and here we go again.
Thinking how time was spent,
    and taking up the pen.

To let you know we're fine,
    yet sparing you details.
We work, we sleep, we dine.
    We tread the same old trails.

But next year brings new things,
    to Europe we soon go.
A three-week dream takes wings.
    We'll soon be out of dough.

For you and your family,
    we hope when this year's done,
all your lives are carefree.
    God bless us everyone!

Christmas, 1996

Christmas Greetings

Why can't I just sit down and write
a note like normal people might?
Just sign our names to save some time
without the wish to pen in rhyme.

It's tough deciding what to say
in order to our year portray.
Add the burden of verse and flow,
my sanity I do forego.

How selfish of me to make you read
this silly poem that meets my need
and puts the weight on you to glean
what the heck it is I mean.

We're fine, we're hale, our kids are near,
we've many hobbies, jobs interfere.
Bought nice big camper for the lake
and often did the grandkids take.

On a pensive note, I must say
we lost Monty's Mom one March day.
Life's dusk came, her sun quickly set,
but in our minds, we see it yet.

We wait for news from those once near.
The time we've shared we still hold dear.
No matter how we keep in touch,
the thought and effort mean so much.

1995

The Gift of the Magi

Christmas comes sooner every year.
Stores determined to bring us cheer.
Halloween now is red and green.
Thanksgiving stuff is hardly seen.
Giving spirit is what we get,
whether or not we want it yet.
If the Magi had brought no gift,
the business world would go adrift.
But Christmas could be as it should.
Just peace and love and all that's good.

The Gift of Time

If I could give a gift to you,
    Would be the gift of time.
More hours each day with naught to do.
    Wouldn't it be sublime?
Time to read, walk, to feel the breeze,
    to talk, to play, to live.
Time is there for you to seize.
    'tis nothing I can give.

A poem written for a Christmas ornament.

Deck the Halls

Deck the halls with boughs of holly,
bought half price in July, by golly.
Tis the season to be jolly
in spite of all the retail folly.

Don we now our gay attire,
found in Kohl's Black Friday mire.
Hear the ancient yule tide choir,
TV jingles that promote desire.

See the blazing yule everywhere.
Stores decorated with a flair.
Strike the harp and join us there,
begging us their shelves to bare.

Follow me with merriness yearned,
spending money that's not yet earned.
While I tell of treasure spurned
as most the gifts will be returned.

Fast away the old year ends—
A nation praised for what it spends.
Hail the new ye human friends.
Do your part as recession pends.

Sing ye joyous of manger shrine,
the meaning of Christmas, we define.
Over us all God's Star doth shine,
even when in a check-out line.

FA LA LA LA LA LA LA LA LA

April 2008

3rd place in the GFWC of KS

www.ingramcontent.com/pod-product-compliance
Lightning Source LLC
Chambersburg PA
CBHW031927090426
42811CB00002B/113